Communicate: ELT lessons for the active classroom

ROBERT KIRKPATRICK

Communicate: ELT lessons for the active classroom, 1st edition
JYUNKO PRESS
Waikato, New Zealand

First published 2012
2015 2014 2013 2012

1 3 5 7 9 10 8 6 4 2

ISBN   978-0-473-11928-7

Table of Contents

· ·

Introduction

The practice sessions in this book almost introduce themselves. By design they need only simple instructions and students can manage the exercises themselves freeing the teacher to walk around the class monitoring pairs, groups and individuals. The materials can be brought into play flexibly to suit different groups at different stages of their development and can be an effective supplement for the longer teaching procedures that make up the main body of an English course.

Who is this book designed for?

The book is designed to help improve the student's understanding and use of language skills by doing tasks and activities using crossword puzzles, dictations, illustrated stories, and roleplays. Copiable, easy-to-use work sheets are suitable for a variety of levels from pre-intermediate to the advanced and also for different ages, children or adults. You, the teacher, are probably the best judge to pick up the appropriate activity in the line with these exercises for your students.

Aims

The aims of this book: a summary

1) To work on the four skills: reading, writing, speaking and listening.
2) To enhance the self-confidence, enjoyment of learning, and creative thinking of the learner.
3) To facilitate learner-centered classrooms.
4) To produce growth in all students, from challenged and non-English language learners to high achievers.
6) To make communicative competence the goal of language teaching.
7) To develop procedures for the four language skills teaching that acknowledge the interdependence of language and communication.

What the book contains

I. Crosswords

Teaching vocabulary to beginners is always difficult; too much vocabulary within little time. Thus helping second language learners build vocabulary by using creative and critical thinking activities to learn words is crucial. By thinking carefully about each word in the crossword "they are forming more connections about the words. This process of thinking about the words helps students remember more vocabulary" (Joanna Szeto, 2010). The method requires students in the classroom to interact with each other in small groups in order to solve the crossword, hence the learning is a collaborative effort. Crosswords activities in the book let students work together (pairs or groups based on class size or their level) to get the right words arranged in the puzzle.

The learners need to speak out, listen to what their partners say, guess, make inferences and draw conclusions based on what they know about each word. The answer will be found through creative thinking, not based on mere memorization. Working in this way, learners are actively engaged in the learning process and deal with their own strengths and weaknesses in English language use.

II. Illustrated stories

Presenting messages and information through illustrations is a significant and rapidly developing medium of communication worldwide. Building up the learner's schema (also pre-knowledge) and drawing meaning upon image and situation, a picture-based approach to teaching language improves creative thinking and language skills through discussions of illustrated pictures as well as encouraging participation and self-confidence.

Of course the abstract and linguistic level given in the stories calls for correspondence with the learners' age and stage. In the case of low-level students the teacher needs to read the stories several times and perhaps simplify the story.

Why use illustrated stories? According to Claudia Connolly (2005):

a) *Working with illustrations provides a creative and artistic learning environment which children respond to.*

b) *A story provides a learner-centred universe where abstract concepts are embodied within the text and pictures.*

c) *A story-based approach can take creative, authentic unadapted texts from all over the world, with their embedded linguistic and artistic cultural identity, to the heart of the language classroom.*

d) *Facilitating pair/group discussions enable students to practice respectful, democratic, collaborative problem solving skills that over time transfer to other classroom interactions.*

e) *Eager, thoughtful participation nurtures learners' verbal language skills, and writing assignments assist transfer from simple oral to complex written ability.*

f) *Stories providing strong messages let language learners gain a sharp sense of contemplation, justice and fairness.*

g) *Children are given tangible tasks where they learn to collaborate with their peers. In this learner-to-learner relationship, children feel more comfortable and can build on their self-confidence and self-esteem in the learning environment.*

III. Dictations

Dictation is an effective language learning tool which has been used for centuries. Attentive listening is at the heart of dictation and "it trains pupils to distinguish sounds; it helps fix concepts of punctuation; it enables pupils to learn to transfer oral sounds to written symbols; it helps to develop aural comprehension; and it assists in self-evaluation" (Finocchiaro, 1969).

Dictation helps to emphasize sentence structures and vocabulary as well as uncovering comprehension and grammatical errors/weaknesses in learners. It ensures that they know what they need to focus more on to improve their listening skills before stepping forward to advanced stage. For teachers, lessons can be prepared to address errors made by a majority of the class, seeing through the result of the strengths and weaknesses of each student. Scott Alkire, (2002) highlighted many advantages of dictation and his points are summarized below:

a) Students and teacher can be aware of the students' comprehension errors phonological, grammatical, or both.
b) Students practice comprehending and transcribing clear English prose.
c) They learn correct forms of speech and perform better in note-taking skills.
d) All four language skills will advance in tandem with each other.
e) No matter how large the class is, every student has to be actively involved.
f) In pre-, during and post-activities, all students are active.
g) Correction can be done by the students if the teacher wishes.
h) Using interesting texts can arouse learners' motivation to study the target language.
i) Students at any level can carry out the tasks based on the exercises they need.
j) Non-native teachers and inexperienced ones can control the whole class comfortably and effectively in language learning environment.
k) Students' overall language ability can be quickly evaluated by their skill in completing the dictations.

Class, pair, and group work

Learners expect lessons and texts to be engaging and motivating, in contrast to the boring techniques they experienced in their school-day lives. Lessons and exercises are generally focused on form through well-prepared textbooks and tests but learning language in the class should also emphasize oral communication through pair- and group-work. Moreover, students do not just come to practice English, but are expected to learn by themselves in the future.

The activities offering in this book mainly focus on pair/group work in the large/small classes and team work skills through creative thinking as well as individual active involvement (eg. presenting as a representative of each group for the illustrated stories lessons and dictations).

✓ *Pair work*
Pair work is easy and fast to organize. It provides opportunities for intensive listening and speaking practice. Pair work is usually better than group work if there are no discipline problems.

✓ *Group work*
Some exercises and activities require four to six players; group work is essential in such cases. If there is to be competition between groups, they should be of mixed ability.

Motivation

Motivation is an integral part of successful language learning. It is learning how to keep on being motivated that is the key to the consistent effort need to become fluent. A great deal of research has studied and pointed out the importance of the use of group activities during teaching

Teachers can create the basic motivational conditions through (Dimitrios Thanasoulas, 2001):

a) *appropriate teacher behaviour and good teacher-student rapport*
b) *a pleasant and supportive classroom atmosphere*
c) *a cohesive learner group characterised by appropriate group norms*
d) *considering that each learner's interests and expectations are different*
e) *cultivating the belief that competence is a changeable aspect of development*
f) *making the learning context less stressful and classroom anxiety lessen*
g) *providing regular experiences of success*
h) *encouraging positive self-assessment*
i) *a small personal word of encouragement*
j) *maintaining and protecting motivation*

> k)   *being aware of uninteresting topics, repetitive activities, and not enough language exposure which can affect the student's learning attitude and motivation*

How to use this book

Follow the instructions mentioned at the beginning of crosswords, illustrated stories and dictation lessons. Suggestions for different situations such as learners' level or class size are also given.

References

Alkire, Scott. (2002, March). Dictation as a language learning device. *The Internet TESL Journal, Vol. VIII,(3)*. Retrieved from http://iteslj.org/Techniques/Alkire-Dictation.html

Connolly, C. (2005, November). *Story books in the classroom.* Retrieved from http://www.teachingenglish.org.uk/think/articles/story-books-classroom

Finocchiaro, M. (1969). *Teaching English as a second language.* (Rev. Ed.) p. 176. New York: Harper & Row.

Szeto, J. (2010, April). Critical thinking activities for the classroom. Retrieved from http://www.suite101.com/content/critical-thinking-activities-for-the-classroom-a221342

Thanasoulas, D. (2001, June). Motivation and motivating in the foreign language classroom. *The Internet TESL Journal, Vol. VII(6)*. Retrieved from http://iteslj.org/Articles/Norris-Motivation.html

1. Crosswords

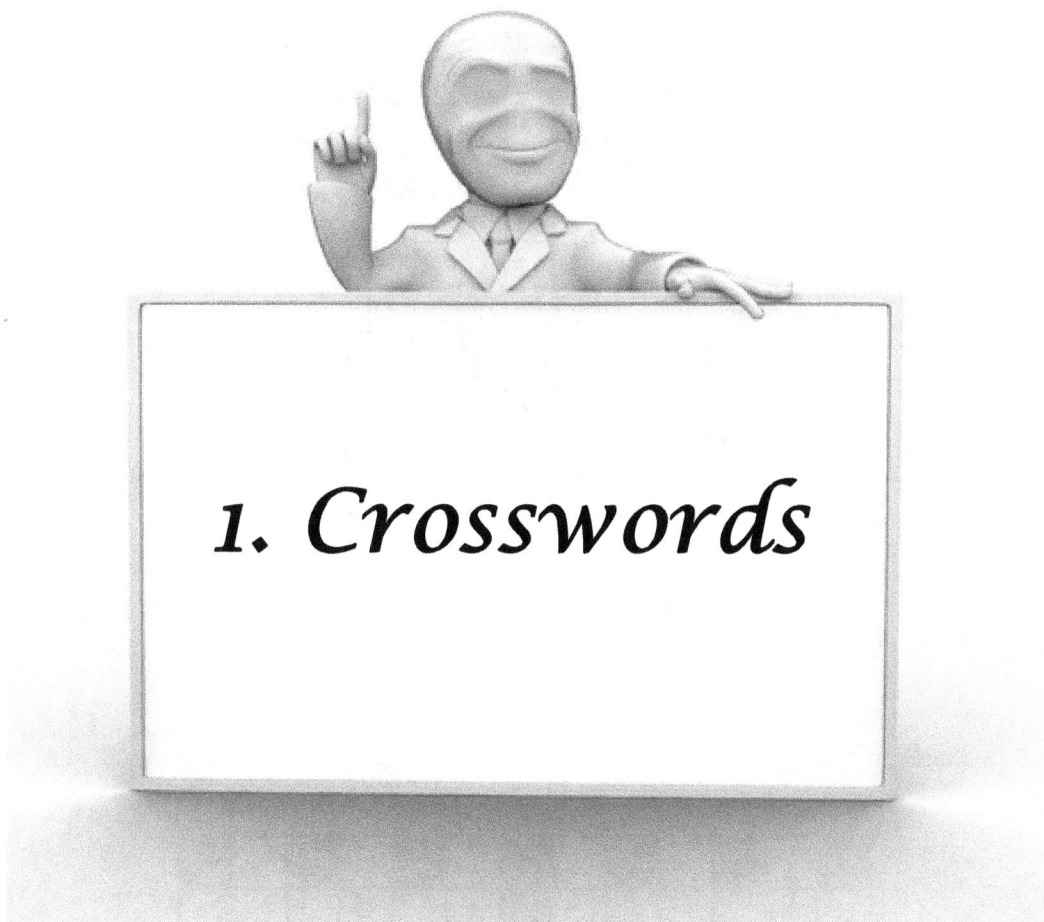

In this section, students work in pairs (or groups). One looks at sheet A and the other sheet B. They give hints **in English** that help the other person guess the word.

Example:
A. What is four down?
B. It is an animal. It lives in our house or outside in kennel. It has 4 legs and says "woof, woof" or barks. It is very loyal.
A. Dog!
B. Yes!

If students are pre-intermediate or above I do it as an A-B exercise. If the level is lower, I put them in small groups. If the class is small, the teacher can be A and let students be B.

If the level is low, tell students they can give the first letter of the word if the other student can't guess after a certain time.

Student A

Crossword 1

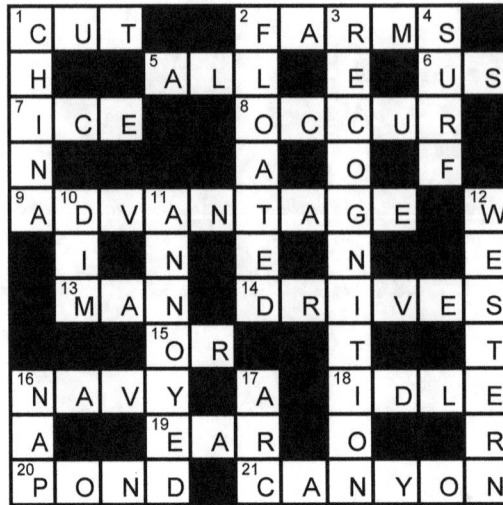

Ask student B for hints.
Example: What is one down?
What is two across?

Crossword 2

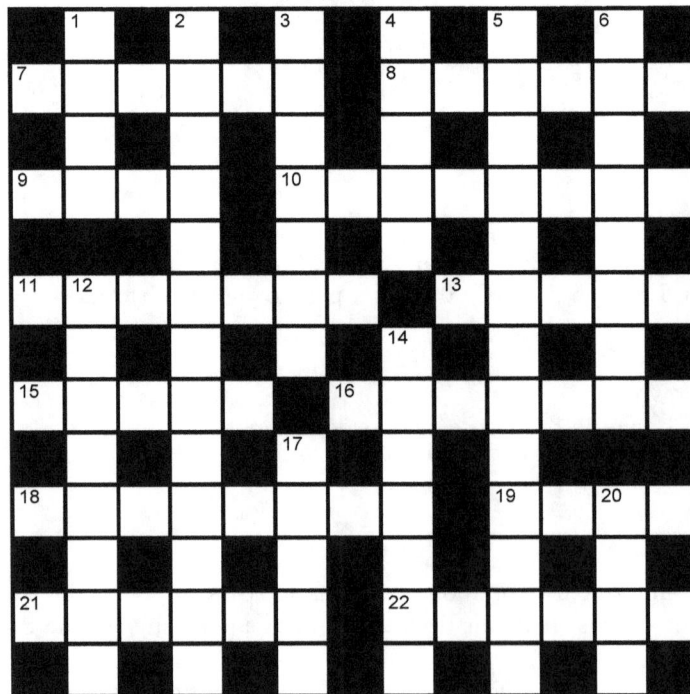

Student B

Crossword 1

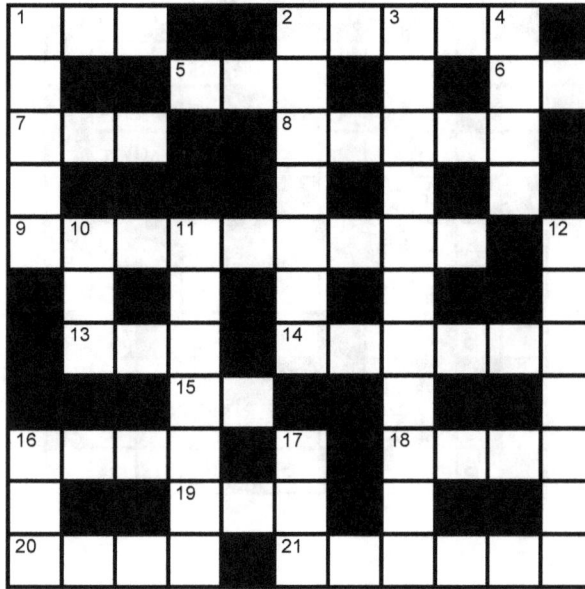

Ask student B for hints.
Example: What is one down?
What is two across?

Crossword 2

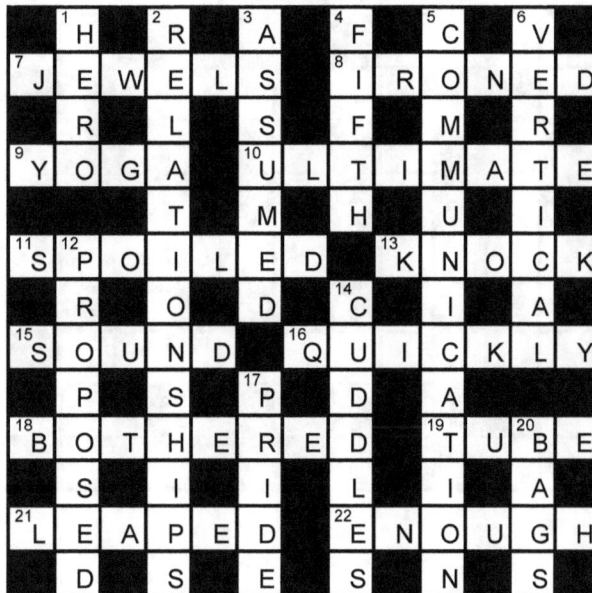

Student A

Crossword 3

								¹D	
²P	A	³R	T	⁴N	E	R	⁵S	H	I	P
I		E		U			P		S	
⁶E	X	C	I	T	E	M	E	N	T	
		I		S			C		⁷I	T
⁸G	A	P					T		N	
R		⁹E	¹⁰N	C	¹¹O	U	R	A	G	E
¹²A	S		O		N		U		U	
B		¹³D	¹⁴O			¹⁵M	A	I	N	
¹⁶S	¹⁷O		¹⁸F	¹⁹I	X			S	
	²⁰R	A	M		F		²¹E	C	H	O

Ask student B for hints.
Example: What is one down?
What is two across?

Crossword 4

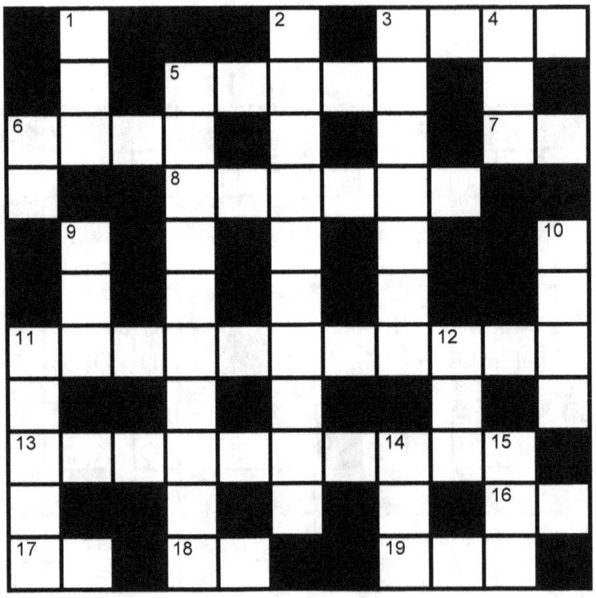

(blank crossword grid with numbered cells 1–19)

Student B

Crossword 3

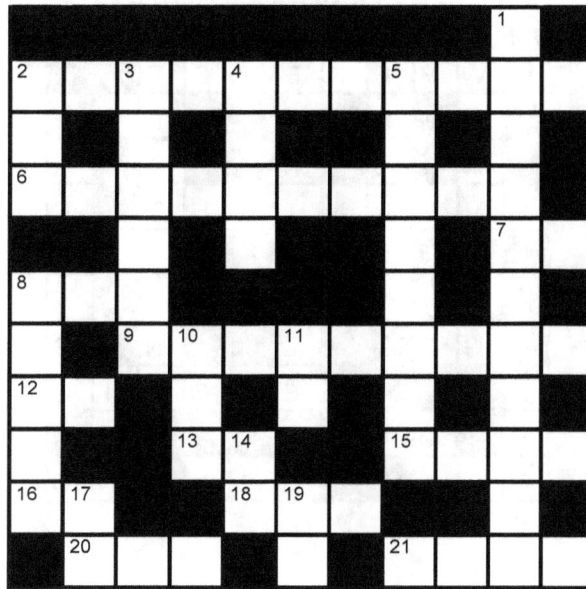

Ask student A for hints.
Example: What is one down?
What is two across?

Crossword 4

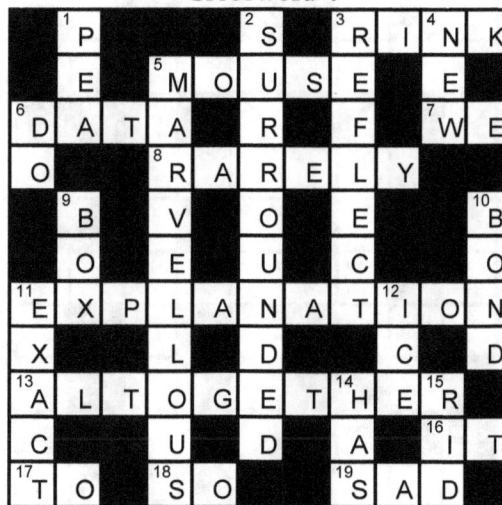

Student A

Crossword 5

				¹M			²T	A	X
	³W	H	⁴E	N	E	V	E	R	
	E		N	A			⁵E	Y	⁶E
	A		E	N			A		A
⁷O	V	E	R	N	I	G	H	T	R
	I		G	N		⁸M	E		
	N		Y		⁹G	I	V	E	¹⁰A
	¹¹G	O			L		N		R
¹²A				¹³E	X	O	T	¹⁴I	C
R		¹⁵O	N	E	S			N	
¹⁶M	E	N		¹⁷S	I	X	¹⁸N	O	

Ask student B for hints.
Example: What is one down?
What is two across?

Crossword 6

Student B

Crossword 5

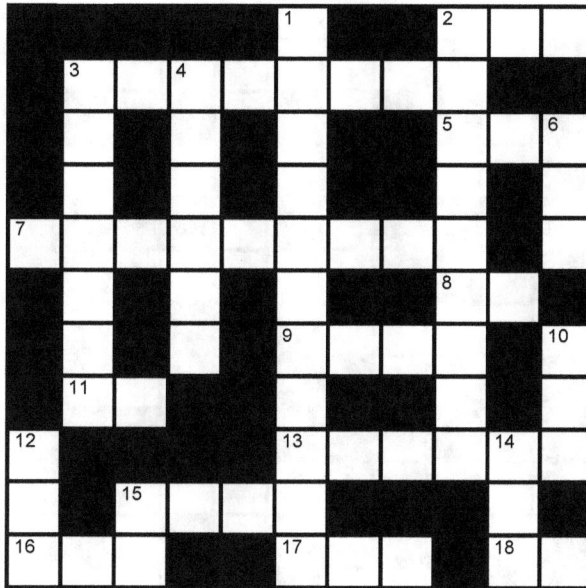

Ask student B for hints.
Example: What is one down?
What is two across?

Crossword 6

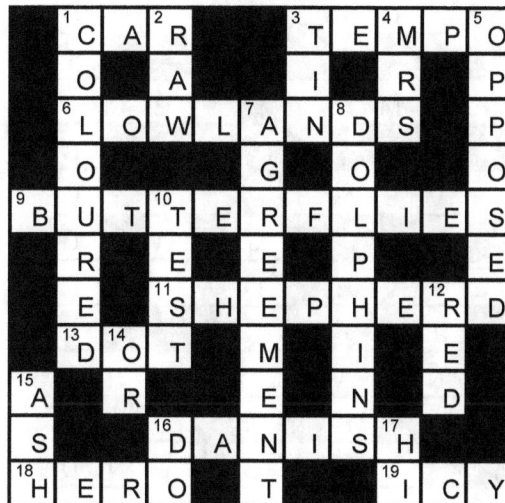

Student A

Crossword 7

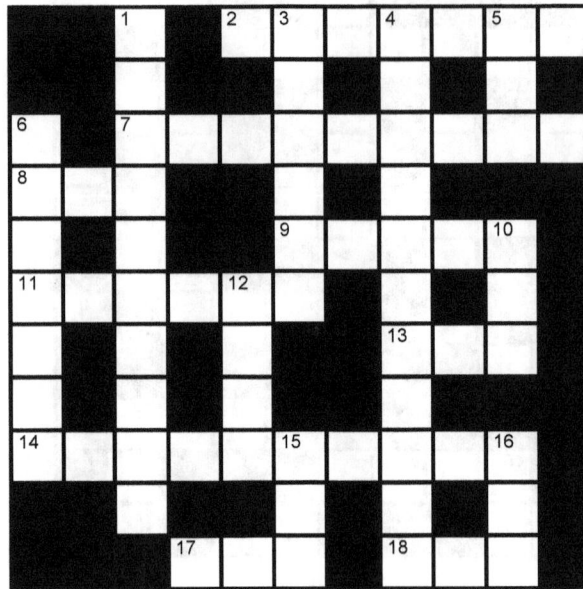

Ask student B for hints.
Example: What is one down?
What is two across?

Crossword 8

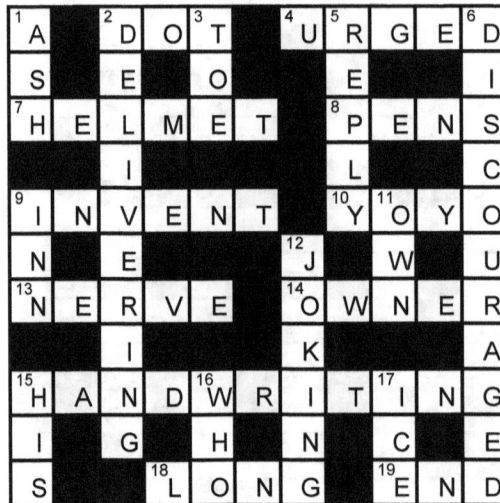

Student B

Crossword 7

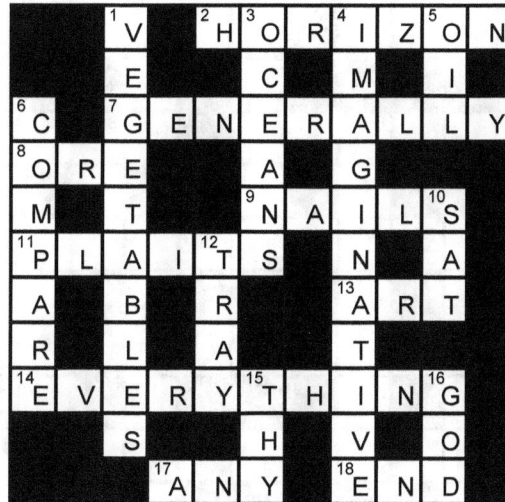

Ask student B for hints.
Example: What is one down?
What is two across?

Crossword 8

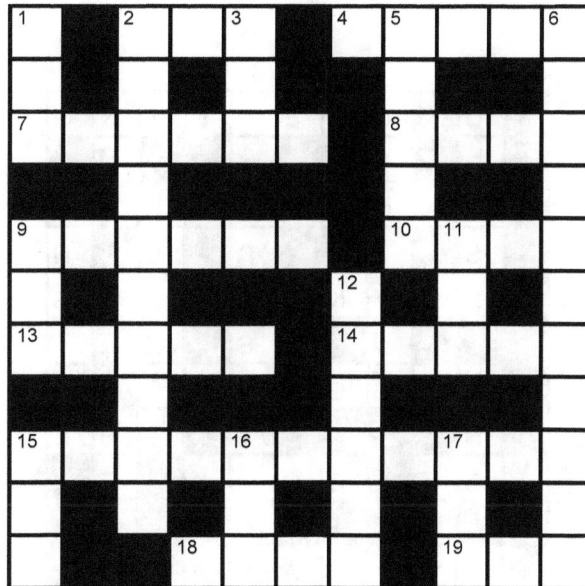

Student A

Crossword 9

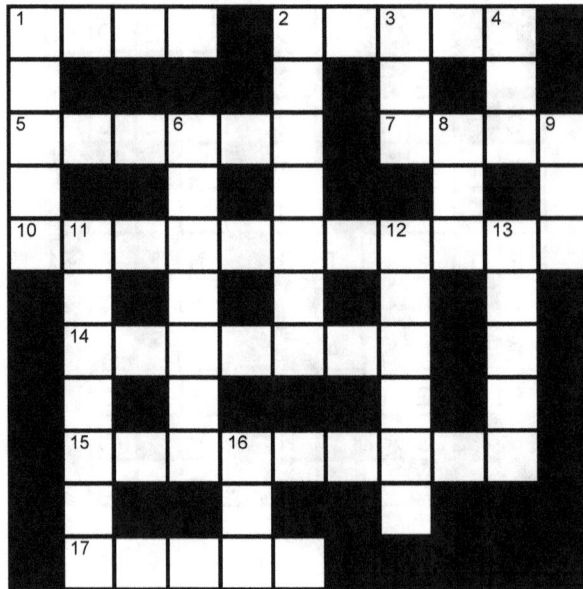

Ask student B for hints.
Example: What is one down?
What is two across?

Crossword 10

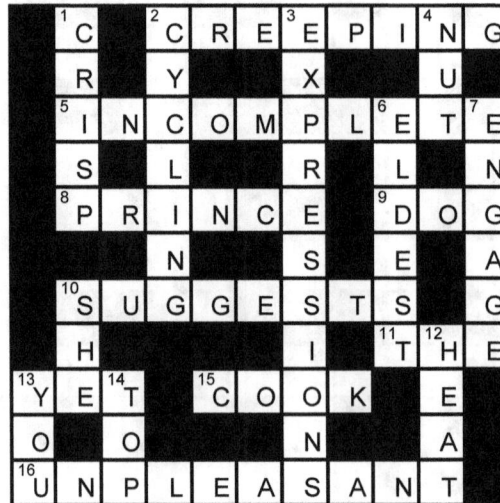

Student B

Crossword 9

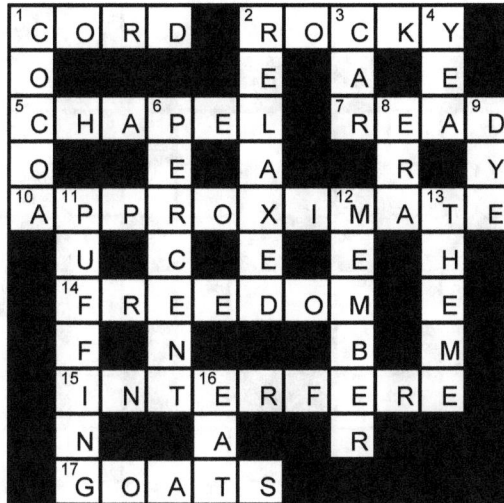

Ask student B for hints.
Example: What is one down?
What is two across?

Crossword 10

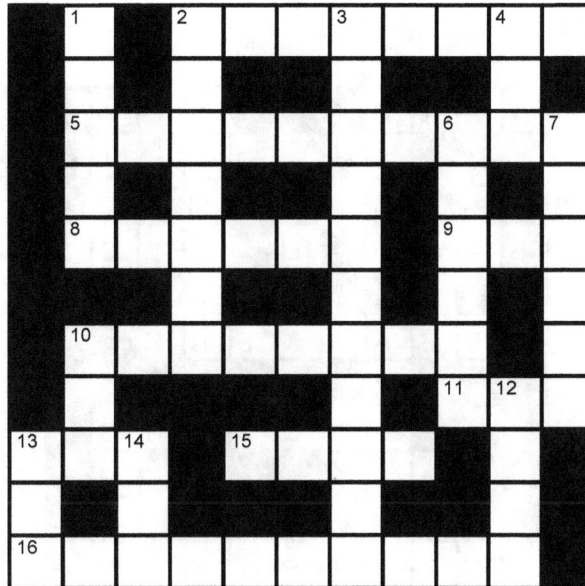

Student A

Crossword 11

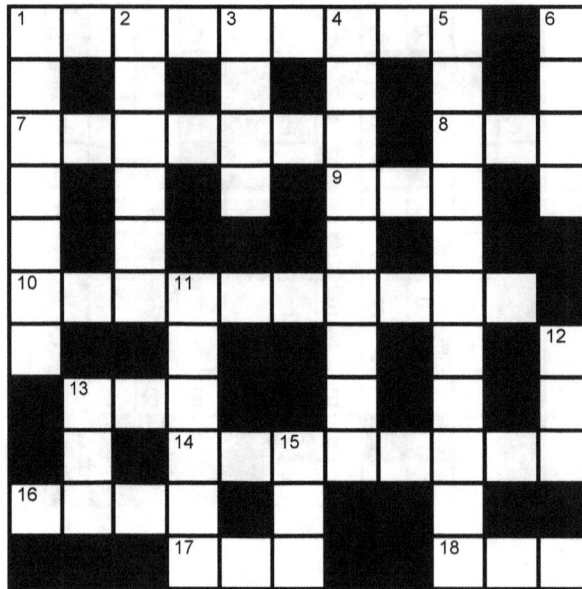

Ask student B for hints.
Example: What is one down?
What is two across?

Crossword 12

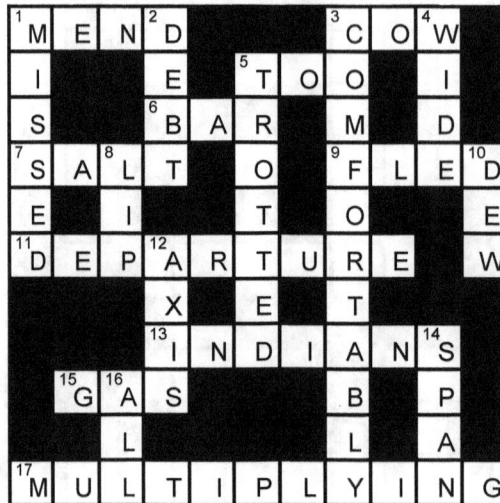

Student B

Crossword 11

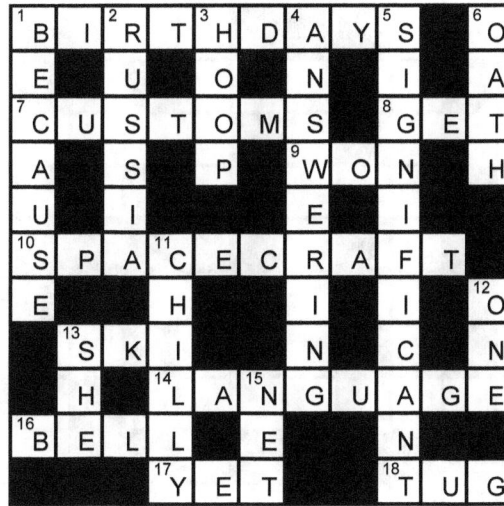

Ask student B for hints.
Example: What is one down?
What is two across?

Crossword 12

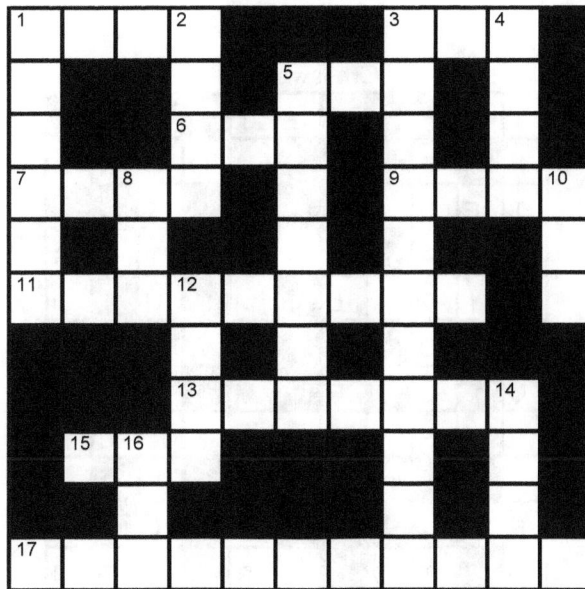

Student A

Crossword 13

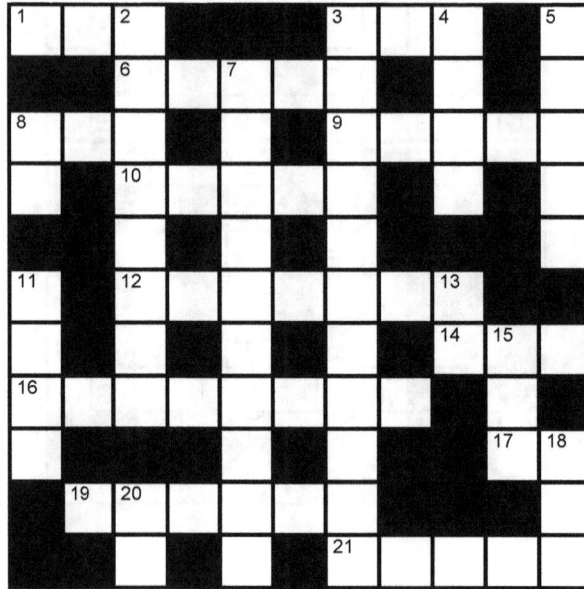

Ask student B for hints.
Example: What is one down?
What is two across?

Crossword 14

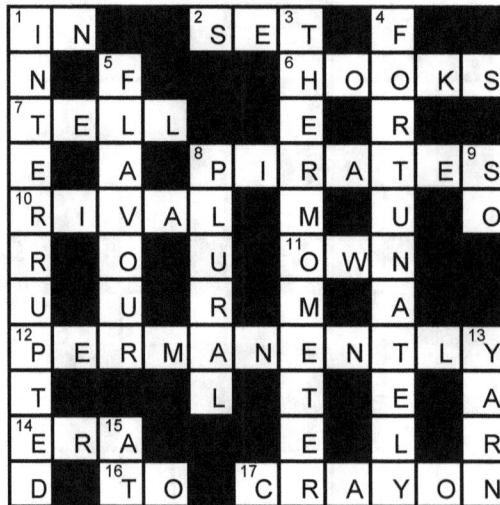

Student B

Crossword 13

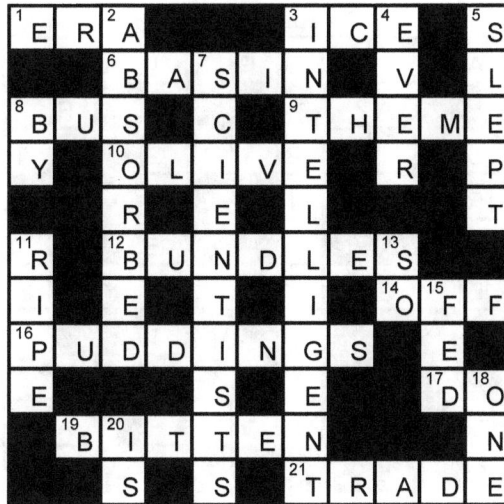

Ask student B for hints.
Example: What is one down?
What is two across?

Crossword 14

Student A

Crossword 15

A¹	P	P²	R	O	P	R	I³	A	T⁴	E
■	■	A	■	■	■	■	N	■	R	■
C⁵	L	I	M	B⁶	I	N	G	■	A⁷	T
R	■	D	■	I	■	■	R	■	P	■
I	■	■	■	C	■	■	E	S⁸	O⁹	■
E¹⁰	V	E¹¹	R	Y	B	O	D	Y	■	F
D	■	A	■	C	■	■	I	■	■	F
■	■	S	■	L	■	E¹²	L	F¹³	■	■
T¹⁴	■	E¹⁵	L	E	V	E	N	■	A¹⁶	N
U	■	L	■	■	■	T	■	■	T	■
B¹⁷	U	S	I	N	E	S	S	M	E	N

Ask student B for hints.
Example: What is one down?
What is two across?

Crossword 16

Student B

Crossword 15

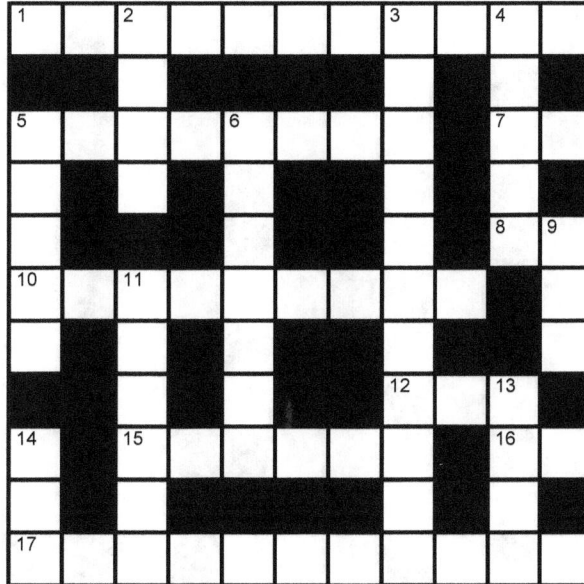

Ask student B for hints.
Example: What is one down?
What is two across?

Crossword 16

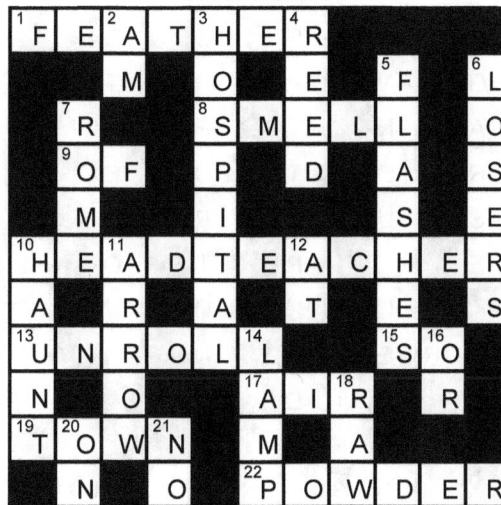

Student A

Crossword 17

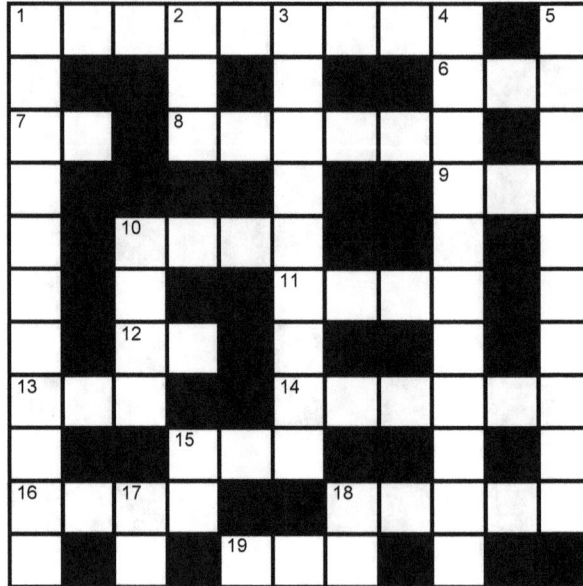

Ask student B for hints.
Example: What is one down?
What is two across?

Crossword 18

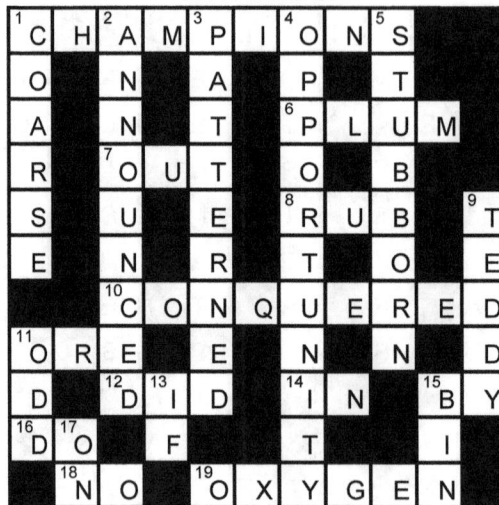

Student B

Crossword 17

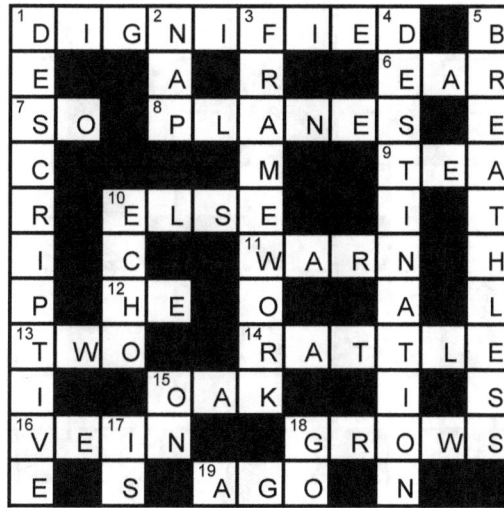

Ask student B for hints.
Example: What is one down?
What is two across?

Crossword 18

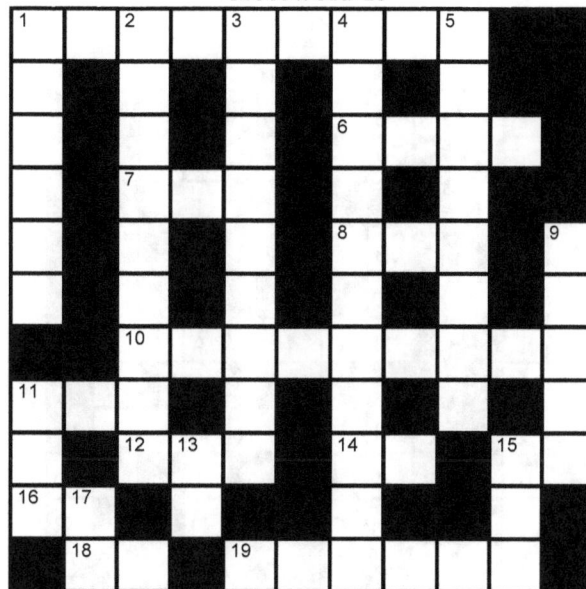

Student A

Crossword 19

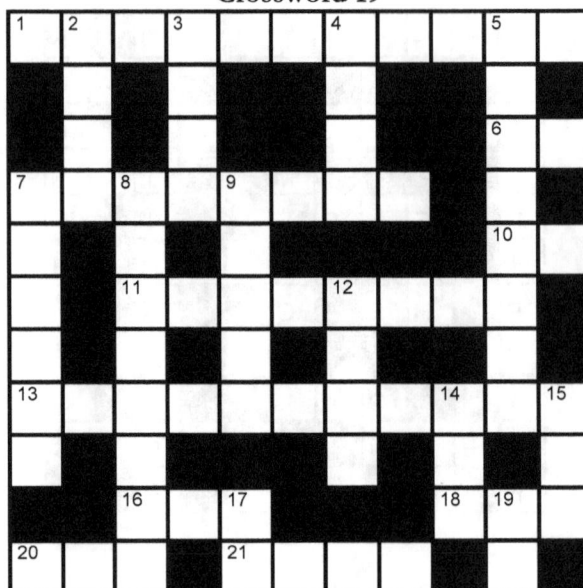

Ask student B for hints.
Example: What is one down?
What is two across?

Crossword 20

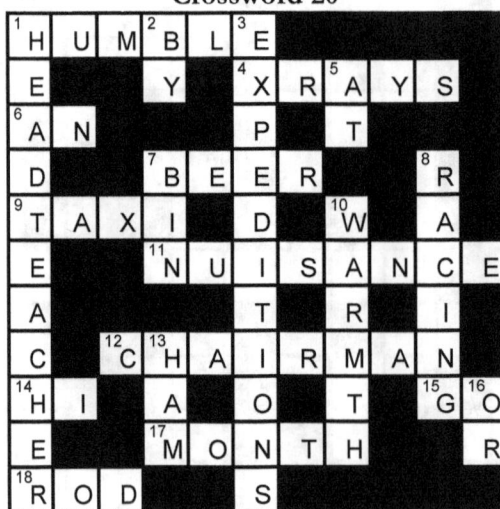

Student B

Crossword 19

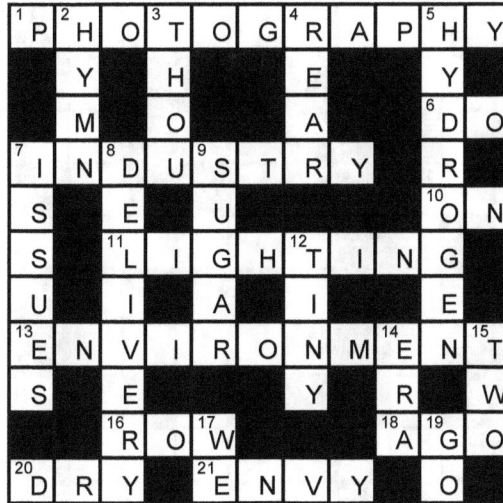

Ask student B for hints.
Example: What is one down?
What is two across?

Crossword 20

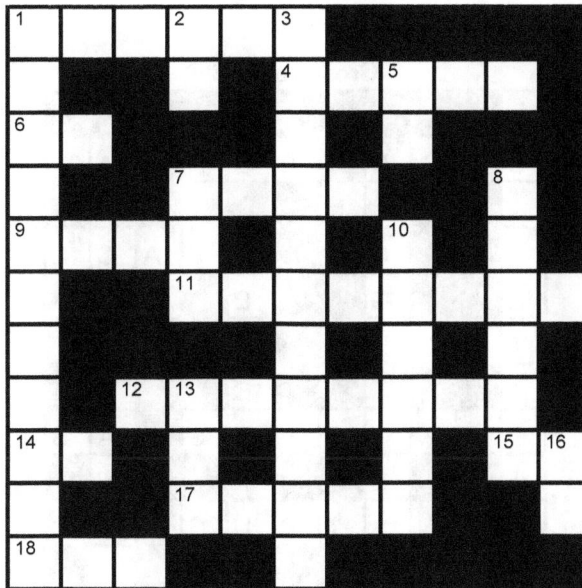

Student A

Crossword 21

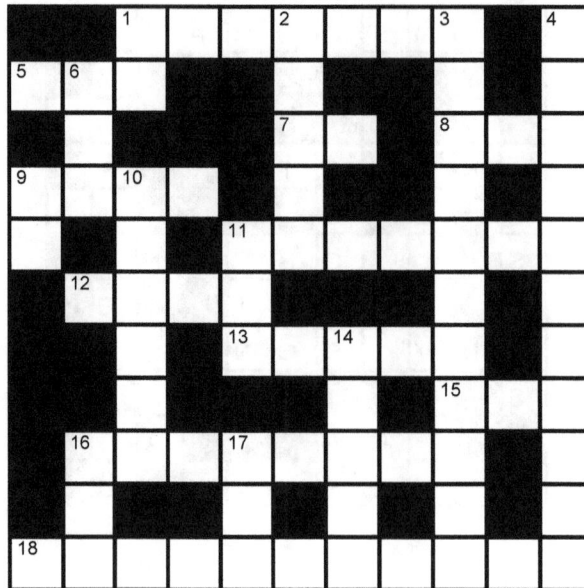

Ask student B for hints.
Example: What is one down?
What is two across?

Crossword 22

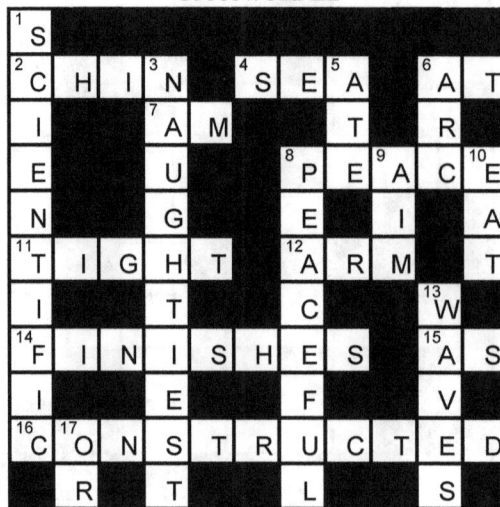

Student B

Crossword 21

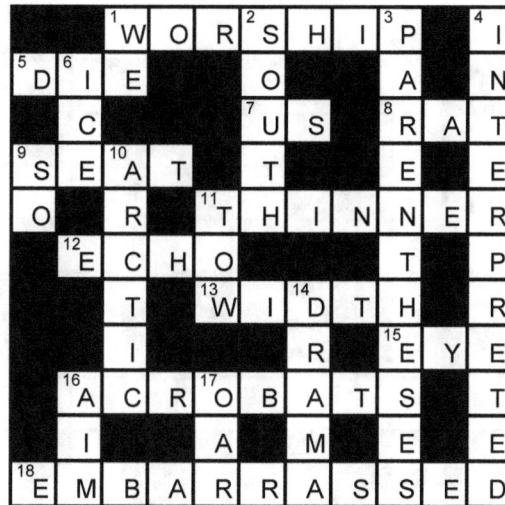

Ask student B for hints.
Example: What is one down?
What is two across?

Crossword 22

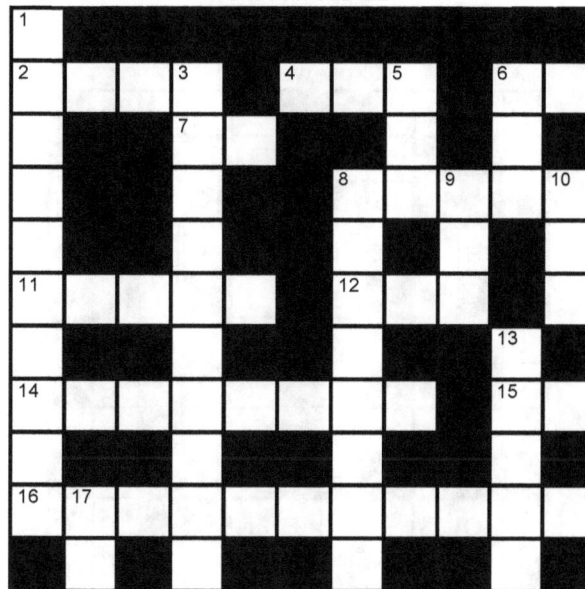

Student A

Crossword 23

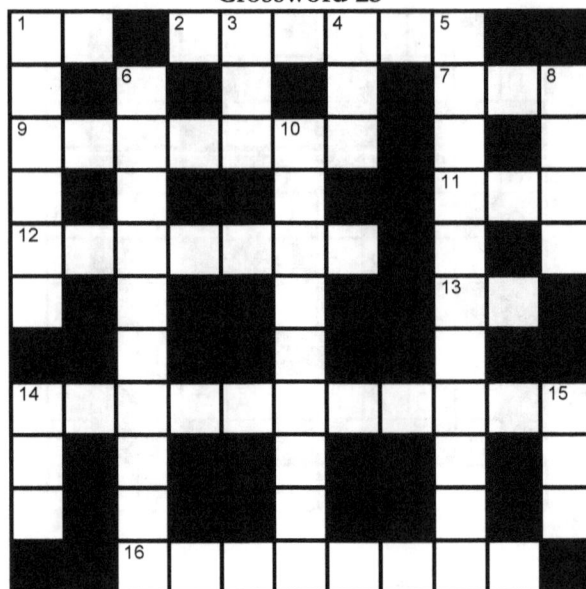

Ask student B for hints.
Example: What is one down?
What is two across?

Crossword 24

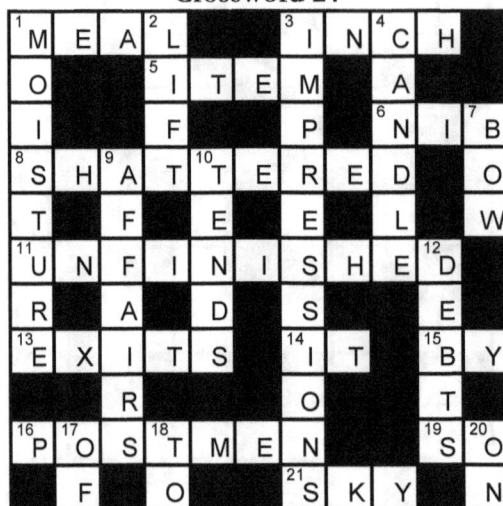

Student B

Crossword 23

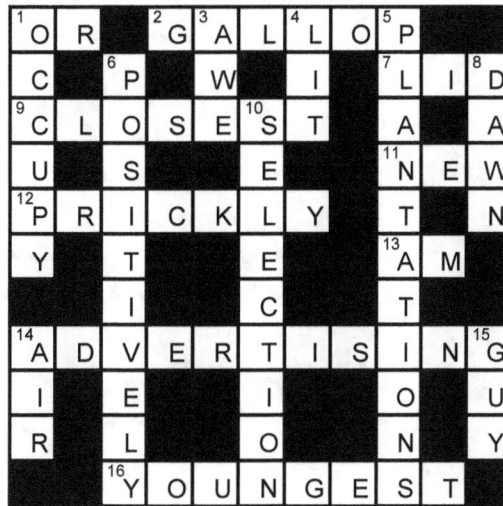

Ask student B for hints.
Example: What is one down?
What is two across?

Crossword 24

2. Illustrated Stories

Step 1. Let the students look at the story pictures then ask them to discuss with their partner what they think the story is about. Chose one or two students to stand up and tell the class their ideas.

Step 2. Read the story. Ask students to take notes and put the story together with their partner or in a group. Repeat until students understand it fairly well. Generally, it is best if they write out the story so that it is easy for the teacher to walk around the class and see how everyone is doing.

Step 3. Ask different students to tell sections of the story.

Step 4. Let students read the story.

Alternative

1. Take two stories and assign one story to half the class and one to the other half. Ask the first half to leave the classroom and then read their story to the remainder.

2. Then send this half out and ask the other half to return. Read the other story. Repeat one or two times.

3. Bring everyone back into the classroom and join group A with group B on a one to one basis. A people tell B people about their story and vice versa.

Check their understanding by walking around the class asking questions.

Story 1

Figure 1

Figure 2

Story 2

Figure 1

Figure 2

Story 3

Story 4

Desert figure 1

Desert figure 2

Desert figure 3

Desert figure 4

_____
_____
_____
_____
_____
_____
_____
_____
_____

_____

Story 5

_____
_____
_____
_____
_____
_____
_____
_____
_____
_____
_____
_____
_____
_____
_____
_____
_____
_____
_____
_____
_____
_____
_____

Story 6

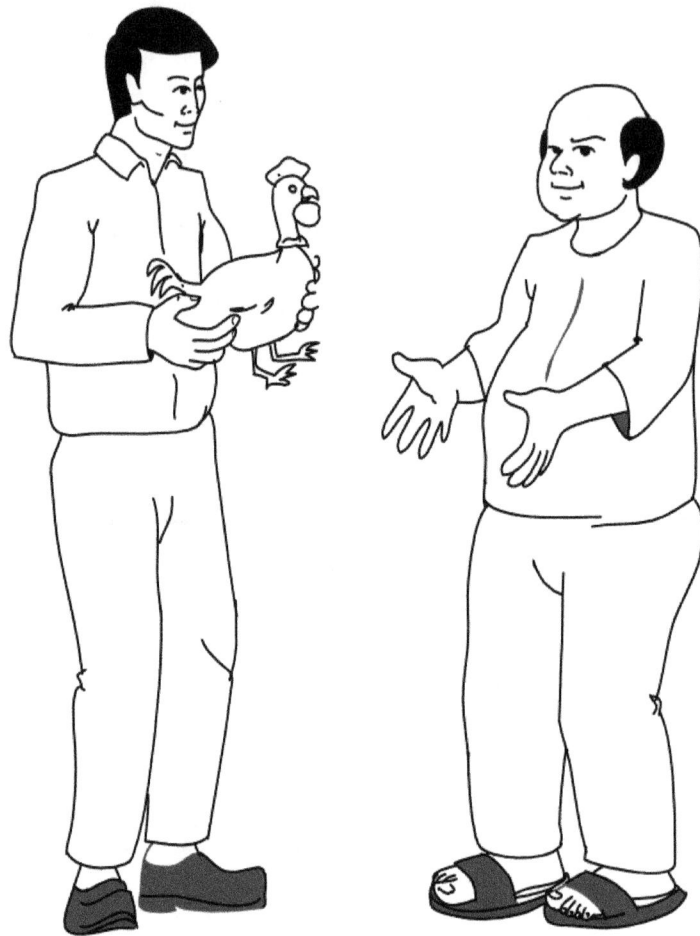

Story 7

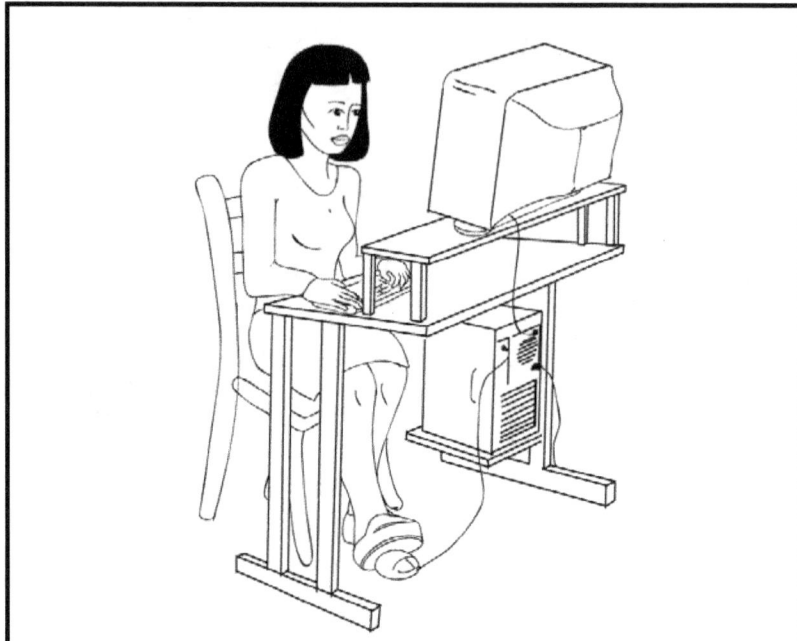

Story 8

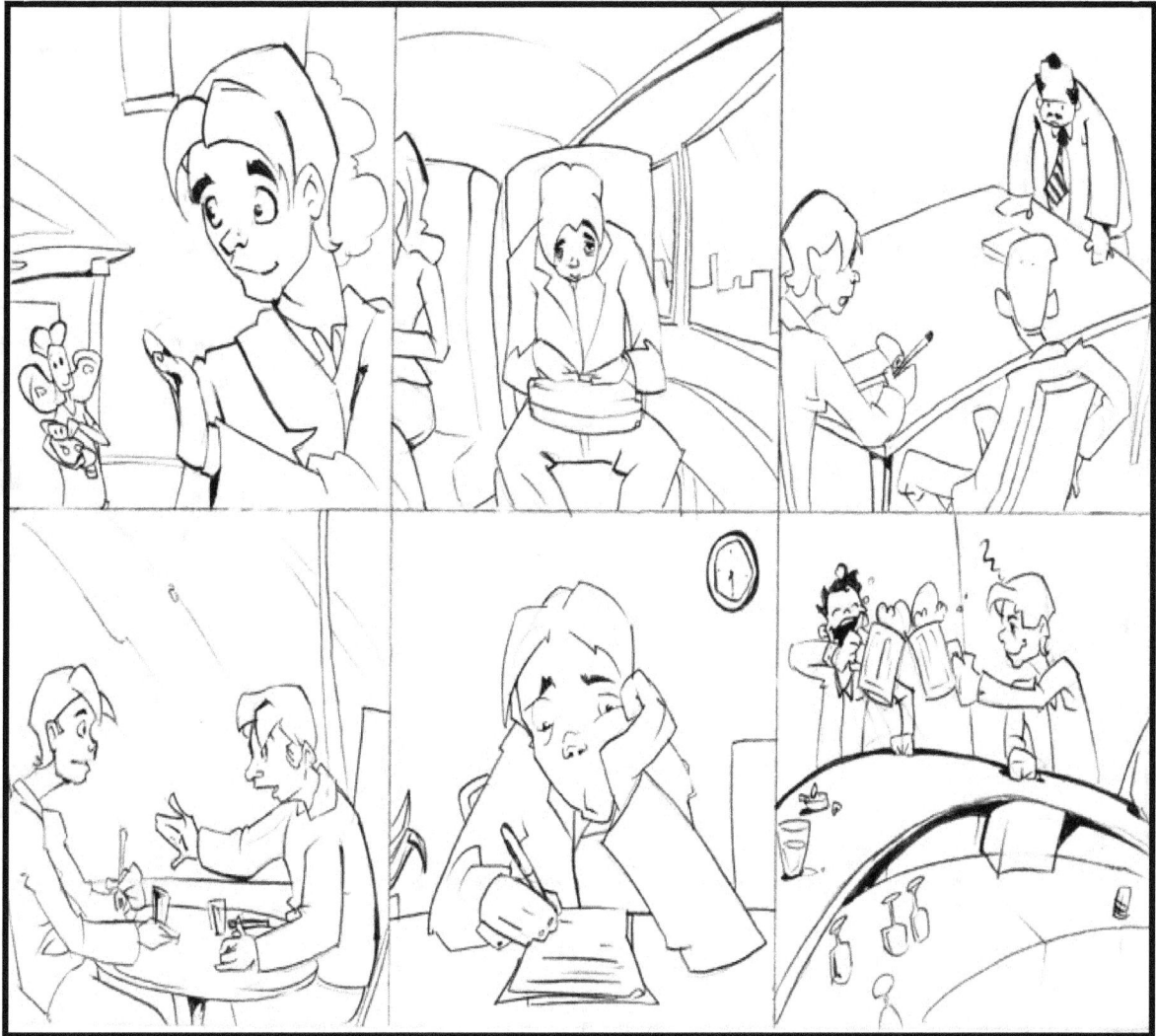

Story 9

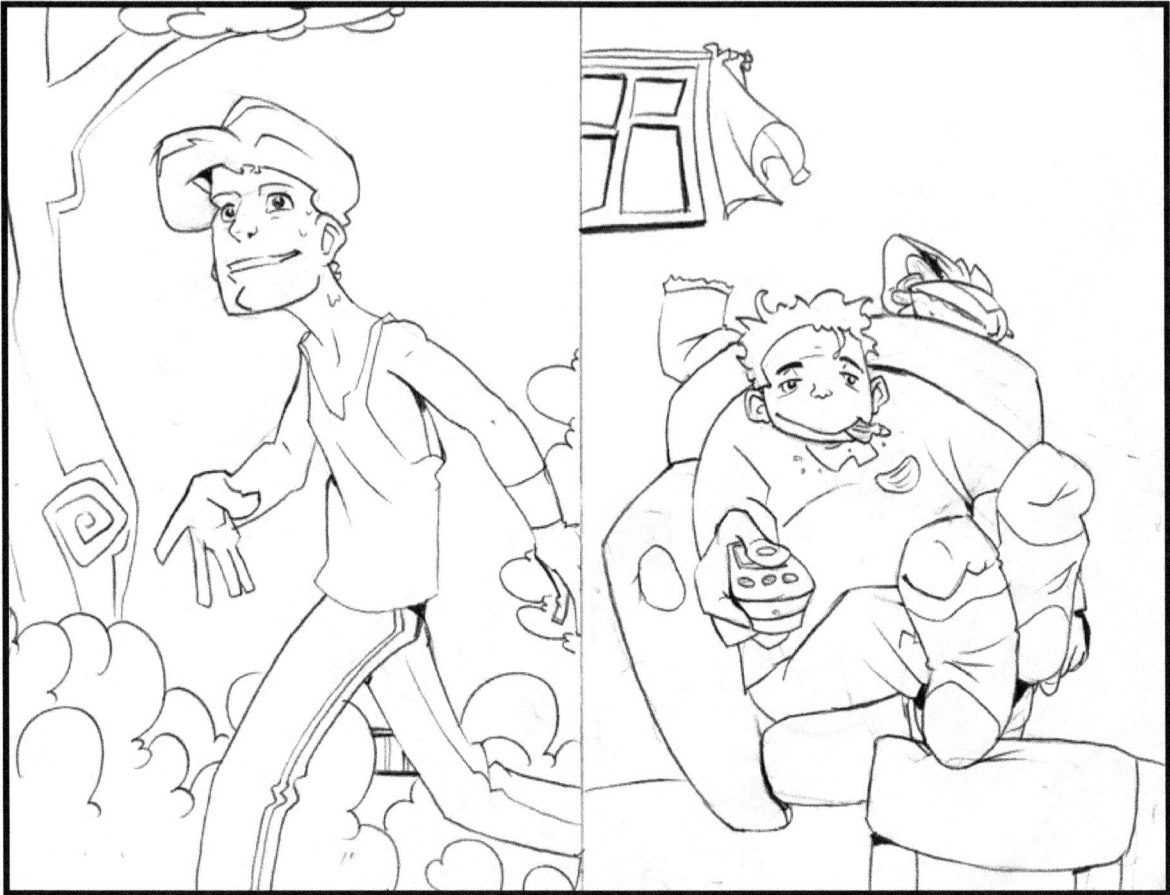

Look at the pictures and compare the two men.

Think of words related to clothes, hobbies, activities, health, and the future.

Prepositions of place

Student B describes to student A where the various kitchen utensils and items are. Student A must draw them on his picture without looking at Student Bs picture.

Student A

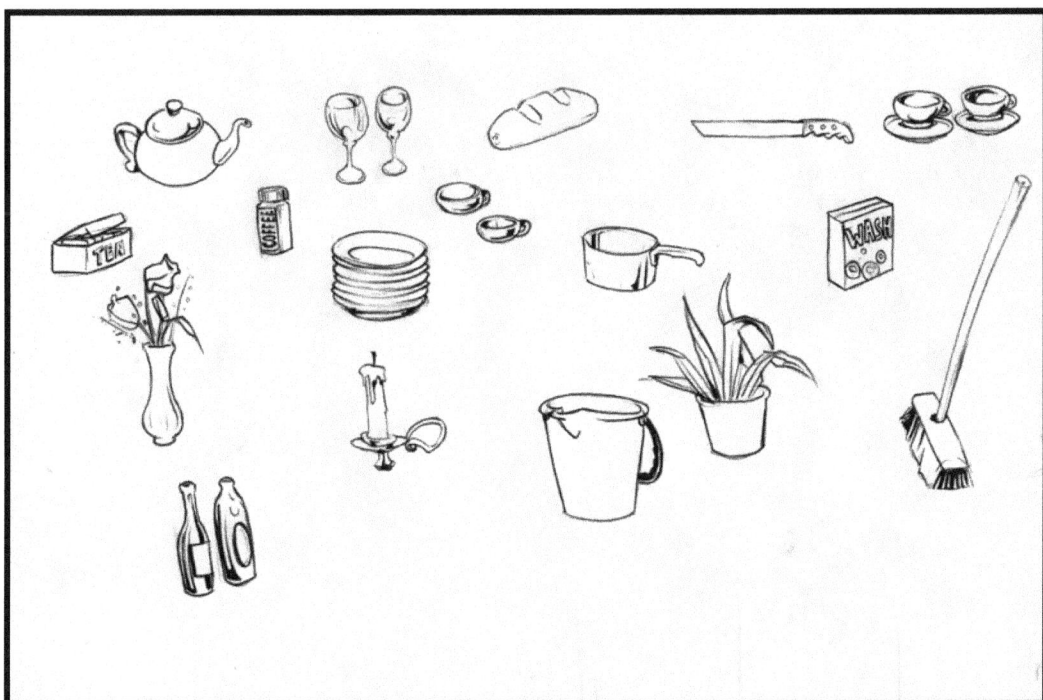

Student B

RECIPE

Possible ways to use the recipe in class:

1. Teacher reads the recipe to class as a dictation.

2. Students look at the pictures and write their own recipe.

3. Student A reads the recipe and Student B writes it out (while looking at the pictures).

Ingredients

- 4 eggs
- Salt & pepper
- 2 tsp olive oil
- onion thinly sliced
- tomatoes, finely chopped
- 5g butter

Recipe

1. Use a fork to whisk eggs and milk together. Season well with salt and pepper. Set aside.

2. Heat oil in a non-stick frying pan over medium high heat. Add onions and cook for 3 to 5 minutes. Then stir in chopped tomato. Cook 1 min. Remove from pan and set aside.

3. Melt a little butter in the frying pan then add eggs to the pan. Continue until egg mix is ready.

4. Spoon onion and tomatoes mixture over half the omelette. Use a fork to lift one side of the omelette over the filling. Carefully put onto serving plate and have with fires or salad.

3. Dictations

Example dictation:

Alcohol _____ Finland officials _____last week. About

_____people died from alcohol related illnesses and almost 1000 _____

Finland _____ and is known for heavy drinking.

Two years ago _____ taxes 40 _____ where alcohol is

_____.

Scripts
Alcohol is the main cause of death in Finland officials said last week. About 2,000 people died from alcohol related illnesses and almost from accidents or violence caused by alcohol. Finland has a population of 5.2 million and is known for heavy drinking. Two years ago the government reduced taxes 40 percent to discourage people going on drinking trips to Russia where alcohol is much cheaper.

Dictation exercises

1) _____, Columbus _____

and discovered it. Copernicus, _____, and

revealed them! No one _____ after he had

triumphed. Instead, _____, thus proving once more that __

_____ NO ALIBIS.

If _____. Put _____

_____ defeat, for _____

_____ SEED _____.

Henry Ford, _____

he possessed, _____

_____ entire earth. _____

_____.

Thomas Edison _____

_____, and despite _____

_____ until he _____

Practical _____.

....

2) Regular _____ might increase _____ depressive episode.

According to _____, people who _____

_____ to experience _____ than colleagues _____

_____ eight-hour work day.

3) _____ Michael Pemberton _____

to an institution in the countryside. _____ sedated _____

_____ café for a break. However to

his horror _____

_____ now empty.

Rather than _____, Michael _____

picking up _____ 20 people in the bus.

He then _____ patients.

_____ _____ "highly excitable."

When _____ the jury heard _____

_____ Michael's cover-up.

....

4) I have often thought it would be _____ if each human _____

_____ a few days at some time during _____. Darkness would make him

_____ sight; silence would teach him _____

_____ sound.

Make the most of _____; glory in _____ which would reveals to you

through _____ which Nature provides. But of all the senses, I am

sure that _____.

5) In 1975, the imprisoned crews of Japanese trawler _____

_____ the truth.

When they were _____ clutching _____

_____ told authorities that _____

_____ of the wreckage.

They were _____. They remained _____

_____and Russian authorities _____

their cargo planes _____ in Siberia, _____

_____.

However, _____get agitated _____

_____ cargo hold. _____

_____ on the trawler.

....

6) The white star liner Titanic, _____, _____ Southampton,

England, _____ to New York City on Wednesday, April 10, 1912. She was built with

_____ and her _____. She was _____.

7) A thirsty fox _____.

Eventually _____

_____ bottom. The fox studied _____

_____, one bucket going down _____

_____. So _____ and

his weight _____, where _____

_____ he desired.

However, _____, but the fox had long ago _____

_____ of fools, and a short time later along _____ in the

well.

The fox _____the goat, 'Get _____

_____ go up.

'Yes, _____,' asked the goat.

'_____, then _____ go down.'

So the goat _____, and in a moment _____

_____, and the fox _____ at the top.

But the fox bade _____.

'Wait_____,' shouted the goat. 'You _____

_____.'

'_____?' asked the fox. '_____possibilities.'

8) Milk: _____. _____ the finding _____

drinking _____ a day _____ brain power.

_____ January issue of _____. Researchers

_____ of Maine _____ scored _____

_____ than those _____. Those with _____

_____ were five times _____ non milk

drinkers.

....

9) In 1985, _____ Julia Weinburg _____

_____ Manchester, UK, _____

regain her figure _____ baby, _____

any day.

She sensed _____, but _____

she attempted _____her shoulder.

A security guard _____ shop, _____

_____ shoplifting a basketball.

Julia _____serious. The

only _____

_____ waters broke. _____

a son.

10) Friends, _____ -- for about _____

_____, Facebook _____ in life.

Think of Facebook _____, virtual of course, _____

_____. Instead of _____

_____ profile picture. _____

_____ funny story _____, but _____

_____ the comments _____

for other people.

Let's have a party

Your teacher will give you a role. Fill in the sheet with extra information. Then memorize the information and move around the class.

Role card 1

Name:_____ (*make up a name*)

You live in a large, expensive apartment in New York. You work as a model for _____ agency. Your age is _____. You didn't go to university and left school when you were 17. Your hobbies are _____.

You (like/hate/love) your job because_____. Your boyfriend/girlfriend is a _____. You like to drink _____.

Make up more details about your life

Role card 2

Name:_____ (*make up a name*)

You are a yakuza boss with many tattoos and a missing finger. Your age is_____ Your hobbies are _____
You (like/hate/love) your job because _____ Your boyfriend/girlfriend is a _____ You like to drink _____

Make up more details about your life

Role card 3

Name:_____ (*make up a name*)

You were released from prison last month after serving 10 years for robbing a bank. You have $500,000 hidden somewhere. Your age is_____ Your hobbies are (apart from guns)_____
You (like/hate/love) your job because _____ Your boyfriend/girlfriend is a _____
You like to drink_____

Make up more details about your life

Role card 4

Name:_____ (*make up a name*)

Your age is_____ Your hobbies are (apart from guns)_____
You (like/hate/love) your job because _____ Your boyfriend/girlfriend is a _____ You like to drink _____

Make up more details about your life

Role card 5

Name:_____ (*make up a name*)

You are a famous scientist in _____.
You graduated from Harvard university
Your age is_____
Your hobbies are (apart from
guns)_____
You (like/hate/love) your job
because_____
Your boyfriend/girlfriend is a
_____
You like to drink_____

Make up more details about your life

Role card 6

Name:_____ (*make up a name*)

You were a bank manager but went to prison
after embezzling 3 million dollars. Now you are
semi-homeless after your wife left you. You are
looking for a rich woman to marry
Your age is_____
Your hobbies are _____
_____
You like to drink_____

Make up more details about your life

Role card 7

Name:_____ (*make up a name*)

You are a rich widow, looking for a husband.
You like younger men.
You wear a mini-skirts and low cut blouse.
Your age is_____50_____
Your hobbies are _____
You like to drink_____

Make up more details about your life

Role card 8

Name:_____ (*make up a name*)

You are a famous sumo wrestler.
Your age is_____
Your hobbies are _____
You (like/hate/love) your job
because_____
Your boyfriend/girlfriend is a
_____
You like to drink_____

Make up more details about your life

Role card 9

Name:_____Beckham_____

You are a very handsome British soccer player.
Your age is_____
Your hobbies are_____
You (like/hate/love) your job
because_____
Your wife is a _moviestar_____
You like to drink_____

Make up more details about your life

Role card 10

Name:_____ (*make up a name*)
You are married with two children. You are a
salaryman for NTT.
Your age is_____
Your hobbies are _____
You (like/hate/love) your job
because_____
Your wife is a _____
You like to drink_____

Make up more details about your life

Role card 11

Name:_____ (*make up a name*)

You are a police detective.
Your age is_____
Your hobbies are _____
You (like/hate/love) your job
because_____
Your boyfriend/girlfriend/husband/wife is a
_____
You like to drink_____

Make up more details about your life

Role card 12

Name:_____ (*make up a name*)

You are a writer but not very successful.
Your age is_____
Your hobbies are _____
You (like/hate/love) your job
because_____
Your boyfriend/girlfriend/husband/wife is a
_____
You like to drink_____

Make up more details about your life

Role card 13

Name:_____ (*make up a name*)

You are a millionaire stocktrader.
Your age is_____
Your hobbies are _____
You (like/hate/love) your job
because_____
Your boyfriend/girlfriend/husband/wife is a
_____

You like to drink_____

Make up more details about your life

Role card 14

Name:_____ (*make up a name*)

You are a good ballerina.
Your age is_____
Your hobbies are (
You (like/hate/love) your job
because_____
Your boyfriend/girlfriend/husband/wife is a
_____

You like to drink_____

Make up more details about your life

Role card 15

Name:_____ (*make up a name*)

You are a homeless person who sneaked into the
party.
Your age is_____
Your hobbies are (apart from
guns)_____
You (like/hate/love) your job
because_____
Your boyfriend/girlfriend/husband/wife is a
_____

You like to drink_____

Make up more details about your life

Role card 16

Name:_____ (*make up a name*)

You are a very good chef and own your own
restaurant
Your age is_____
Your hobbies are (apart from
guns)_____
You (like/hate/love) your job
because_____
Your boyfriend/girlfriend/husband/wife is a
_____

You like to drink_____

Make up more details about your life

Role card 17

Name:_____ (*make up a name*)

Your age is_____
Your hobbies are (apart from
guns)_____
You (like/hate/love) your job
because_____
Your boyfriend/girlfriend/husband/wife is a
_____

You like to drink_____

Make up more details about your life

Role card 18

Name:_____ (*make up a name*)

Your age is_____
Your hobbies are (apart from
guns)_____
You (like/hate/love) your job
because_____
Your boyfriend/girlfriend/husband/wife is a
_____

You like to drink_____

Make up more details about your life

Role card 19

Name:_____ (*make up a name*)

Your age is_____
Your hobbies are (apart from
guns)_____
You (like/hate/love) your job
because_____
Your boyfriend/girlfriend/husband/wife is a
_____

You like to drink_____

Make up more details about your life

Role card 20

Name:_____ (*make up a name*)

Your age is_____
Your hobbies are (apart from
guns)_____
You (like/hate/love) your job
because_____
Your boyfriend/girlfriend/husband/wife is a
_____

You like to drink_____

Make up more details about your life

Role card 21

Name:_____ (*make up a name*)

Your age is_____
Your hobbies are (apart from guns)_____
You (like/hate/love) your job because_____
Your boyfriend/girlfriend/husband/wife is a _____

You like to drink_____

Make up more details about your life

Role card 22

Name:_____ (*make up a name*)

Your age is_____
Your hobbies are _____
You (like/hate/love) your job because_____
Your boyfriend/girlfriend/husband/wife is a _____

You like to drink_____

Make up more details about your life

Role card 23

Name:_____ (*make up a name*)

Your age is_____
Your hobbies are (apart from guns)_____
You (like/hate/love) your job because_____
Your boyfriend/girlfriend is a _____

You like to drink_____

Make up more details about your life

Role card 24

Name:_____ (*make up a name*)

Your age is_____
Your hobbies are (apart from guns)_____
You (like/hate/love) your job because_____
Your boyfriend/girlfriend is a _____

You like to drink_____

Make up more details about your life

Other Pairwork/Groupwork Activities

Pair Work

Organize the students into groups with two members. Ask them to discuss certain topics, perform roles or describe few things within their group.

Exercise 1

Student A tells only good things about the forest and Student B speaks only of bad things in the forest. Student A says forest is good because (read to your partner and ask to fill in)

There are many trees	that helps the rain to
There are many animals	
Flowers in the forest	are beautiful and
Forest has caves	
No houses in forest	so that we cannot sleep and
We can eat only	
Small streams in the forest	gives fresh water and
The roads in the forest	

Student B says forest is bad because (read to your partner and ask to fill in)

There are many trees	
There are many animals	that attack humans and
Flowers in the forest	
Forest has caves	wherein thieves stay and
No houses in forest	
We can eat only	raw food and
Small streams in the forest	
The roads in the forest	very difficult to travel and

Exercise 2
Student A and B recall together the school environment

Student A identifies 8 things inside the school building and asks student B to describe them

Objects   Description

Student B identifies 8 things outside the school building and asks student A to describe them

Objects   Description

Exercise 3
Student A and B are talking about their parents' jobs

Parents' job details	Student A	Student B
Father's job		
Mother's job		
Father's work place		
Mother's work place		
Father's qualifications		
Mother's qualifications		
Father's industry		
Mother's industry		

Now, student A and B will answer questions based on each other's parents' job details
To Student B. (Please answer in full sentences.)

Who is Student A's father?
Who is Student A's mother?
Where does Student A's father work at?
Where does Student A's mother work at?
What is the education of Student A's father?
What is the education of Student A's mother?
What is the industry Student A's father works in?

To Student A (Please answer in full sentences)

Who is Student B's father?
Who is Student B's mother?
Where does Student B's father work at?
Where does Student B's mother work at?
What is the education of Student B's father?
What is the education of Student B's mother?
What is the industry Student B's father works in?

Exercise 4

Student A and B alternatively play the roles of teacher and student and discuss about home works.
At first, Student A is teacher.

Why homework is important? Five reasons.
    1. _____
    2. _____
    3. _____
    4._____
    5. _____

Based on the reasons, Student B raises 5 Doubts.
    1. _____
    2. _____
    3. _____
    4._____
    5. _____

Now, Student B is teacher.

Why homeworks is important? Five reasons.
    1. _____
    2. _____
    3. _____
    4._____
    5. _____

Based on the reasons, Student A raises 5 Doubts.
    1. _____
    2. _____
    3. _____
    4._____
    5. _____

Exercise 5

Student A and B lists their experience of visiting super markets?

How super markets are different from ordinary grocery shops?
(Always answer in full sentences)

Student A
1. _____
2. _____
3. _____
4. _____
5. _____

Student B
1. _____
2. _____
3. _____
4. _____
5. _____

Describe the process of buying things from a super market?

Student A
1. _____
2. _____
3. _____
4. _____
5. _____

Student B
1. _____
2. _____
3. _____
4. _____
5. _____

Name five types of employees in a super market and describe their duties

Student A
1) _____
2) _____
3) _____
4) _____
5) _____

Student B
1) _____
2) _____
3) _____
4) _____
5) _____

64   *Dictations*

Name five things you cannot buy from a super market and state the reasons

Student A

1. _____
2. _____
3. _____
4. _____
5. _____

Student B

1) _____
2) _____
3) _____
4) _____
5) _____

Exercise 6

Student A and B portray their favorite pets.
(Both students must complete the sentences orally)

My pet is a _____.
I like my pet because_____.
My pet's color is _____.
My pet usually eats_____.
Having a pet helps to _____.

Exercise 7

Student A and B talk about Sunday.
(Both students must complete the sentences orally)

I like Sundays because _____.
I do not like Sundays because _____.
Next Sunday, I will go to _____ and _____.
My parents _____on Sunday.
Sunday is good if _____.

STUDENT A

The president of America is taking an overseas trip.
Work with your partner (by asking questions) to fill in the spaces. This is a speaking exercise so do **not** let your partner see your paper.

COUNTRY	CITY	REASON FOR VISIT and PERSON HE MEETS	DATE
FRANCE	PARIS		July1-3
		1.Meet the Queen 2. Visit his daughter who is at university in Oxford.	JULY 3 -4
Russia	Moscow		
Iraq		1. Meet with American Military chiefs. 2. Meet with Embassy officials.	
Saudi Arabia			July12-13
South Korea	Seoul		

Possible questions

What city is he visiting next? What dates is he going to be in _____? Why does he go to _____?

STUDENT B

The president of America is taking an overseas trip.
Work with your partner (by asking questions) to fill in the spaces. This is a speaking exercise so do **not** let your partner see your paper.

COUNTRY	CITY	REASON FOR VISIT and PERSON HE MEETS	DATE
		Ask the French Prime minister to send soldiers to a war in the Middle east.	
ENGLAND	LONDON		
		Meet with the president of Russia. Challenge him to a Vodka drinking competition..	
	Baghdad		July 7-10
	Riyadh	1.Ask Saudi king to increase oil production. 2.Study the Koran.	
		Discuss strategy (with the president of South Korea) to use with North Korea.	July14-16

Possible questions

What city is he visiting next? What dates is he going to be in _____? Why does he go to _____?

Scripts for Illustrated Stories

Story 1

One day Nasruddin repaired tiles on the roof of his house. While Nasruddin was working on the roof, a stranger knocked the door.

"What do you want?" Nasruddin shouted out.

"Come down," replied stranger, "So I can tell it."

Nasruddin unwilling and slowly climbed down the ladder.

"Well!" replied Nasruddin, "what was the important thing?"

"Could you give little money to this poor old man?" begged stranger.

Tired Nasruddin started to climb up the ladder and said, "Follow me up to the roof."

When both Nasruddin and beggar were upside, on the roof, Nasruddin said, "The answer is no!"

Story 2

There were two pigs who were brothers. They lived with an old lady who fed them well and treated them very kindly. One day a group of men came to visit the lady and they all drank a great deal. After a few hours the men got hungry and asked the lady to cook something. She was poor and only had enough to feed herself. The men saw the pigs and asked if they could kill the little one to eat. The lady refused saying they were like her children, but after much entreaties she agreed.

The lady called out for the small pig "little brother" to come to her. He started to walk towards the lady but then turned and ran back to his elder brother saying that the woman had a strange look in her eyes. He started to shake. His older brother said to him not to be afraid.

"All beings must die, whether young or old. We are bred for our flesh. Do not fear death my brother, it is better to go calmly."

The men and lady heard this speech and were greatly moved. Throwing away their knives they became sober and the two pigs were left to live a long life.

Story 3

One day Mullah Nasruddin lost his ring down in the basement of his house, where it was very dark. There being no chance of his finding it in that darkness, he went out on the street and started looking for it there under the street lamp. Somebody passing by stopped and enquired.

"What are you looking for, Mullah Nasruddin? Have you lost something?"

"Yes, I've lost my ring."

"Ok I will help you look."

After a long time looking the man asked Mullah, "Where do you think you dropped it?

"In the basement of my house."

But Mullah Nasruddin, "why don't you look for it down in the basement where you have lost it?" asked the man in surprise.

"Don't be silly, man! How do you expect me to find anything in that darkness!"

Story 4: The Desert

Once a time a trading caravan was crossing a large desert. Due to carelessness he didn't notice one night that the camels had turned around while everyone was sleeping. In the morning he headed in the wrong direction. Finally checking his way he realised his mistake and turned the caravan back in the right direction.

But by this time everyone was tired and they had used up their water. The men in the group cried that "All our water is gone, we are lost." So saying, each man flung himself down in despair beneath his own cart. The leader thought to himself, "If I give in, everyone will die."

So he walked until he came on a clump of-grass and thought "where there is grass there must be water." So he ordered a spade to be brought and a hole to be dug. After many hours the hole was deep but they hit upon a large rock and everybody wanted to give up. But the leader feeling sure there must be water under that rock, descended into the hole and studied the rock and said to a serving-lad, "Go down into the hole with this hammer, and strike the rock."

The boy struck the rock and split it and water flowed out. The men and animals drank and bathed and then went on with their journey. They sold their goods at great profit and continued on their happy lives.

Adapted from the Vannupatha Jataka

Story 5: The Story of the Rabbit

Many years ago, when Brahmadatta was ruling India, a rabbit was talking with his friends, jackal, otter, and monkey. The rabbit was very industrious and moral and always told his friends to keep the five precepts and to give gifts whenever they could.

All his friends listened carefully and vowed to do as the rabbit had instructed.

Because of the intensity of virtue of the rabbit and his friends, the throne that Sakka sits on got hot. Sakka is King of the gods and his throne heats up whenever anyone on earth does special good deeds. Feeling the heat Sakka surveyed the earth and listened to the rabbit's words. He wondered how good the rabbit really was and decided to test him.

Sakka took shape as an old wandering monk and came to earth near the rabbit and his friends. Seeing him the otter offered some dried fish that he had found a few days ago. The jackal offered some dried meat that he had been storing and the monkey some bananas he had found in the forest.

However the rabbit had only grass, and he thought to himself. "Men cannot eat grass, what can I give this monk?"

He then vowed to give up his own body and jumped into the fire that the monk was warming himself on. Thinking that by this the monk would be able to eat his flesh once it was cooked. However, this fire was a special fire made by Sakka's magic and the rabbit felt only cool and was not burned.

Seeing this great sacrifice Sakka was greatly impressed and proclaimed the virtues of the rabbit far and wide. Furthermore, he told his architect to sculpt an image of the rabbit into the surface of the moon, so all would remember his valiant deed.

And to this day at full moon we can see the image of the rabbit in the moon.

Adapted from Jataka 316

Story 6: The Fighting Rooster

There once was a man who wanted his fighting rooster to be more ferocious. He took the rooster to a trainer. In a few weeks' time, he returned and saw that his rooster didn't squawk as loudly.

"Not ready yet," said the trainer. Two weeks later he saw that his rooster barely raised his neck feathers and wings.

"Not ready yet," said the trainer. Another week passed. His rooster looked as tame and docile as a chick.

"You've ruined my fine fighting bird!" screamed the man at the trainer.

"Not at all," the trainer replied, "See how calm and secure he is, how serenely strong he stands today. The other fighting birds take one look at him and they all run away.

A Taoist Tale by Chuang Tzu

Story 7: BEFUDDLED PC USERS FLOOD HELP LINES, AND NO QUESTION SEEMS TO BE TOO BASIC

The exasperated help-line caller said she couldn't get her new Dell computer to turn on. Jay Ablinger, a Dell Computer Corp. technician, made sure the computer was plugged in, and then asked the woman what happened when she pushed the power button.

"I've pushed and pushed on this foot pedal and nothing happens," the woman replied.

"Foot pedal?" the technician asked.

"Yes," the woman said, "this little white foot pedal with the *on* switch."

The "foot pedal," it turned out, was the computer's mouse, a hand-operated device that helps to control the computer's operations.

"A frustrated customer called, who said her brand new Computer would not work. She said she had unpacked the unit, plugged it in, opened it up and sat there for 20 minutes waiting for something to happen. When asked what happened when she pressed the power switch, she asked, 'What power switch?'"

Seemingly, simple computer features baffle some users. So many people have called to ask where the "any" key is when "Press Any Key" flashes on the screen that Compaq is considering changing the command to "Press Return Key."

Some people can't figure out the mouse. Tamra Eagle, an AST technical support supervisor, says one customer complained that her mouse was hard to control with the "dust cover" on. The cover turned out to be the plastic bag the mouse was packaged in. Dell technician Wayne Zieschang says one of his customers held the mouse and pointed it at the screen, all the while clicking madly. The customer got no response because the mouse works only if it's moved over a flat surface.

From the Wall Street Journal, Tuesday, March 1, 1994.

Story 8: Salaryman Life in Japan

In the morning the man says goodbye to his family and then catches a train to his job in the city. At his office he has many meetings and then at lunchtime he goes with a friend to a coffee shop. He keeps working until 7:30 pm. Later him and his co-workers might relax at a bar or karaoke.

Scripts for Dictations

1) Let us not forget, Columbus dreamed of an Unknown world, risked his life on the existence of such a world, and discovered it. Copernicus, the great astronomer, dreamed of a multiplicity of worlds, and revealed them! No one denounced him as "impractical" after he had triumphed. Instead, the world worshipped at his shrine, thus proving once more that "SUCCESS REQUIRES NO APOLOGIES, FAILURE PERMITS NO ALIBIS."

If the thing you wish to do is right, and you believe in it, go ahead and do it! Put your dream across, and never mind what the people say if you meet with temporary defeat, for they do not know that EVERY FAILURE BRINGS WITH IT THE SEED OF AN EQUIVALENT SUCCESS.

Henry Ford, poor and educated, dreamed of a horseless carriage, went to work with what tools he possessed, without waiting for opportunity to favor him, and now evidence of his dream belts the entire earth. He has put more wheels into operation than any man who ever lived, because he was not afraid to back his dreams.

Thomas Edison dreamed of a lamp that could be operated by electricity, began where he stood to put his dream into action, and despite more than ten thousand failures, he stood by that dream until he made it a physical reality. Practical dreamers DO NOT QUIT!

(Think and Grow Rich, Napoleon Hill)

2) Regularly working long hours in the office might increase your risk of a serious depressive episode. According to findings published in a scientific journal on Wednesday, people who regularly work 11 hours or more each day are more than twice as likely to experience a major episode of depression than colleagues who stick with an eight-hour work day.

(AFP Relax – Sat, Jan 28, 2012)

3) Bus driver Michael Pemberton was driving 20 patients from an inner city psychiatric hospital to an institution in the countryside. As the patients were sedated, Michael thought it would be all right to stop at a roadside café for a break. However to his horror, he returned to find that every single one of the patients had escaped and the bus was now empty.

Rather than admit to his mistake, Michael decided to cover up what had happened and drove round the city, picking up people from the bus-stops along the way until he had 20 people in the bus. He then drove out to the countryside institution and told them that he was delivering the inner city patients. He also warned the staff that the patients were "highly excitable." When the case later came to court, a jury heard that it took eight hours before the 'patients' managed to convince the institution staff of Michael's cover-up.

(Committed Worker, Incredible Urban Legends: Stranger than Fiction Modern Tales, 2005)

4) I have often thought it would be a blessing if each human being were stricken blind and deaf for a few days at some time during his early adult life. Darkness would make him more appreciative of sight; silence would teach him the joys of sound.

Make the most of every sense; glory in all the sides of pleasure and beauty which the world reveals to you through the several means of contact which Nature provides. But of all the senses, I am sure that sight must be the most delightful.

(Reader's Digest: Classic Collection 2011)

5) In 1975, the imprisoned crews of a Japanese trawler were set free after it was discovered that they were speaking the truth. When they were found in the Sea of Japan clutching the remains of their ship, every single crew member told authorities that a cow falling from the sky had been the cause of the wreckage.

They were immediately arrested. They remained in prison until word of the case go out and Russian authorities admitted that the pilot of one of their cargo planes had stolen a cow from the edge of airfield in Siberia, and put the creature on his plane before taking off.

However, when the cow began to get agitated, the crew pushed the animal out of the cargo hold. The animal fell 30,000 feet before landing on the trawler

(An Unlikely Story, Incredible Urban Legends: Stranger than Fiction Modern Tales, 2005)

6) The white star liner Titanic, the largest ship the world had ever known, sailed from Southampton, England, on her maiden voyage to New York City on Wednesday, April 10, 1912. She was built with double bottoms, and her hull was divided into 16 watertight compartments. She was thought to be unsinkable.

(Reader's Digest: Classic Collection 2011)

7) A thirsty fox was wandering about the countryside looking for water. Eventually he found a well, but the only water was at the bottom. The fox studied the problem and realized that there was a pulley system to bring up the water, one bucket going down causing another bucket to come up. So the fox jumped into the bucket at the top and his weight immediately caused it to drop to the bottom, where he could drink all the water he desired.

However, now he could not get back up, but the fox had long ago realized that the world is full of fools, and a short time later along came a goat, looking for water in the well.

The fox explained the situation and said to the goat, 'Get into the bucket, then you can come down and I can go up.'

'Yes, but what about afterwards?' asked the goat.

'That's even simpler; then you can come up and I'll go down.'

So the goat got into the bucket, and in a moment he was at the bottom of the well, and the fox was at the top. But as soon as he was up, the fox bade farewell to the goat and made to leave.

'Wait a minute,' shouted the goat. 'You promised to get me back up.'

'Who promised?' asked the fox. 'All we did was to discuss the possibilities.'

(The fox and the Goat, 366 Fairy Tales, 2010)

8) Milk: it does a brain good. At least that's the finding of a new study that suggests drinking a glass of milk a day could boost your brain power.

In the study published in the January issue of the *International Dairy Journal*, researchers at the University of Maine found that adults who consumed more dairy products scored "significantly" higher on memory and other cognitive tests than those who drank little to no milk. Those with high milk intake were five times less likely to fail the test compared to non milk drinkers.

(AFP Relax – Tue, Jan 31, 2012)

9) In 1985, mother-to-be Julia Weinburg was browsing in a sports shop in Manchester, UK, looking for some sports equipment to help her regain her figure after the arrival of her baby, that was due any day.

She sensed someone was following her, but it was not until she attempted to leave the store that she felt a hand on her shoulder.

A security guard asked her to step back inside the shop, where he and the store manager took her to a back room and accused her of shoplifting a basketball.

Julia laughed at first, but became upset when she was realized that they were serious. The only way of proving that she was not a thief was to show them her stomach, which she was about to do when her waters broke. This soon settled the matter, and nine hours later Julia gave birth to a son.

(Bumpy Times, Incredible Urban Legends: Stranger than Fiction Modern Tales, 2005)

10) Friends, soulmates, lost parents, not to mention work opportunities -- for about 10 percent of the planet, Facebook is where you go to find much of what matters most in life.

Think of Facebook as something like a 24-hour party, virtual of course, with a chance to meet your friends' friends. Instead of spotting someone across the room, you'll first see them in their profile picture. You might not hear them telling a funny story to a group in the corner of the room, but you could easily be enticed by the comments they put up on their page or that of other people.

(Online news: http://www.bangkokpost.com/tech/computer/277958/love-friends-work-how-facebook-changes-life)